THE OFFICIAL ENGLAND ANNUAL 2019

A Grange Publication

© 2018. Published by Grange Communications Ltd., Edinburgh, under sublicence from Panini UK Ltd.

Printed in the EU.

Photographs © PA Images

ISBN 978-1-912595-06-8

CONTENTS

WORLD CUP
ACCESS ALL AREAS

Fitness Tests

Training

Meeting Fans

Press Conference

Tunisia Vs England

Having Fun

Exploring

England vs Panama

Harry Kane Hat-Trick

Recovery

England vs Belgium

England vs Colombia

England
vs Sweden

3rd Place
Play-off

ENGLAND WORDFIT

Can you fit the England World Cup 2018 squad into this grid?

ALEXANDER-ARNOLD	ALLI	POPE	WELBECK
HENDERSON	KANE	ROSE	PICKFORD
LOFTUS-CHEEK	DIER	CAHILL	TRIPPIER
LINGARD	JONES	STONES	WALKER
MAGUIRE	VARDY	YOUNG	STERLING
RASHFORD	DELPH	BUTLAND	

Answers on p.60

SPOT THE DIFFERENCE

Can you spot the ten differences in this photo of Dele Alli scoring the second goal in England's winning game against Sweden during the FIFA World Cup quarter-final match?

Answers on p.60

ENGLAND ROOM MATES

Jesse on Marcus

1. What minute did M score on his England debut?

A) 3rd
B) 4th
C) 5th

Jesse says: "Should I know this? I'm going to go for C, 5th!"

> **You say:**

2. Who is Marcus' musical guilty pleasure?

A) The Weeknd
B) Stefflon Don
C) Childish Gambino

Jesse says: "I tell you, none of them are guilty pleasures. I'll say Stefflon Don!"

> **You say:**

3. What is Marcus' worst habit?

A) Talking while eating
B) Biting his nails
C) Snoring

Jesse says: "Ha ha! You should see his nails – B, nails!"

> **You say:**

4. What area in Manchester was Marcus born in?

A) Rusholme
B) Trafford
C) Wythenshawe

Jesse says: "C, Wythenshawe."

> **You say:**

5. What did Marcus and Neymar talk about in the tunnel at Wembley?

A) The weather
B) London nightlife
C) Nike boots

Jesse says: "He knows nothing about the London nightlife, so I'm going to go for C, Nike boots."

> **You say:**

Jesse's Final Score: 2/5

Marcus on Jesse

1. What is Jesse's football boot size?
A) 7 1/2
B) 8
C) 8 1/2
Marcus says: "I'm gonna go for 7 1/2. Or is it 8? Nah, it's 7 1/2."

You say:

2. Who is Jesse's sporting hero?
A) Cristiano Ronaldo
B) Floyd Mayweather
C) Paul Scholes
Marcus says: "I'm gonna say Scholesy. It's a tough one – the other two are probably more iconic but I know he's always really admired the way Scholesy used to play."

You say:

3. Which team does Jesse's cousin Gabby George play for?
A) Everton
B) Chelsea
C) Blackpool
Marcus says: "Er, A – Everton."

You say:

4. Who sings the song, 'Lingard'?
A) Mostack
B) Malachi Amour X Manzo
C) Young T & Bugsey
Marcus says: "I know this one, you know. 'Lingard...' Oh, I'm just going to guess between B and C. I'm going to go for B."

You say:

5. Which team did Jesse do the Pied Piper dance against?
A) Arsenal
B) Leicester
C) Middlesbrough
Marcus says: "I'm going to go for Leicester."

You say:

Marcus' Final Score: 3/5

WINNER!

DESIGN YOUR OWN ENGLAND KIT

There's nothing better than seeing the latest England kit launch, so why not have a go at creating your own England home and away kits?

Check out some of the classic and crazy kits below, and then have a go yourself! Grab your coloured pens or pencils and design new kits for Gareth Southgate's team!

CLASSIC HOME KITS

1984-85

1997-99

1990-92

2011-12

1995-96

AWESOME AWAY KITS

1996

2016

2000

2018-20

NOW IT'S YOUR TURN!

AWAY

HOME

20 QUESTIONS!

Think you know it all about England? Then try this quiz!

1. Who is England's all-time record goalscorer?

2. Which player has won more caps – Harry Maguire or John Stones?

3. Which world-famous brand produces England's kit?

4. How many times have England won the World Cup?

5. Before 2018, when was the last time they reached a World Cup semi-final?

6. Who made their England debut first – Harry Kane or Dele Alli?

7. Who had the most England players at the World Cup – Tottenham or Manchester City?

8. How many World Cup penalty shootouts have England ever won?

9. Which colour kit did England play in against Croatia in the World Cup semi-final?

10. Who has scored more goals for England – Marcus Rashford or Jamie Vardy?

11. Which player is the record cap holder for England?

12. What is the capacity of Wembley Stadium?

13. Who scored England's first goal of the 2018 World Cup?

14. How many goals did England score at the 2018 World Cup?

15. Which player is taller – Marcus Rashford or Danny Welbeck?

16. Who scored England's first goal in the World Cup quarter-final against Sweden?

17. And who scored the opening goal of the semi-final against Croatia?

18. Which club have Gary Cahill and Fabian Delph both played for?

19. How many goals did John Stones score at the 2018 World Cup?

20. True or False? Harry Kane was the top scorer at World Cup 2018.

Answers on p.60

FACE IN THE CROWD

Can you spot the ten England players hiding in this Three Lions crowd? They're all in here somewhere!

Answers on p.61

19

PLAYER PROFILES

GOALKEEPERS
JACK BUTLAND
JORDAN PICKFORD
NICK POPE
DEFENDERS
TRENT ALEXANDER-ARNOLD
GARY CAHILL
PHIL JONES
HARRY MAGUIRE

DANNY ROSE
JOHN STONES
KIERAN TRIPPIER
KYLE WALKER
ASHLEY YOUNG
MIDFIELDERS
DELE ALLI
FABIAN DELPH
ERIC DIER

JORDAN HENDERSON
JESSE LINGARD
RUBEN LOFTUS-CHEEK
FORWARDS
HARRY KANE
MARCUS RASHFORD
RAHEEM STERLING
JAMIE VARDY
DANNY WELBECK

JORDAN PICKFORD

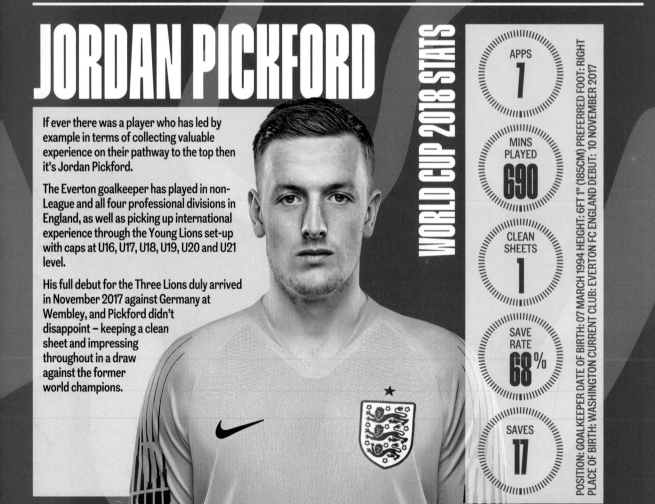

If ever there was a player who has led by example in terms of collecting valuable experience on their pathway to the top then it's Jordan Pickford.

The Everton goalkeeper has played in non-League and all four professional divisions in England, as well as picking up international experience through the Young Lions set-up with caps at U16, U17, U18, U19, U20 and U21 level.

His full debut for the Three Lions duly arrived in November 2017 against Germany at Wembley, and Pickford didn't disappoint – keeping a clean sheet and impressing throughout in a draw against the former world champions.

WORLD CUP 2018 STATS

APPS
7

MINS PLAYED
690

CLEAN SHEETS
1

SAVE RATE
68%

SAVES
17

POSITION: GOALKEEPER DATE OF BIRTH: 07 MARCH 1994 HEIGHT: 6FT 1" (185CM) PREFERRED FOOT: RIGHT
PLACE OF BIRTH: WASHINGTON CURRENT CLUB: EVERTON FC ENGLAND DEBUT: 10 NOVEMBER 2017

JACK BUTLAND

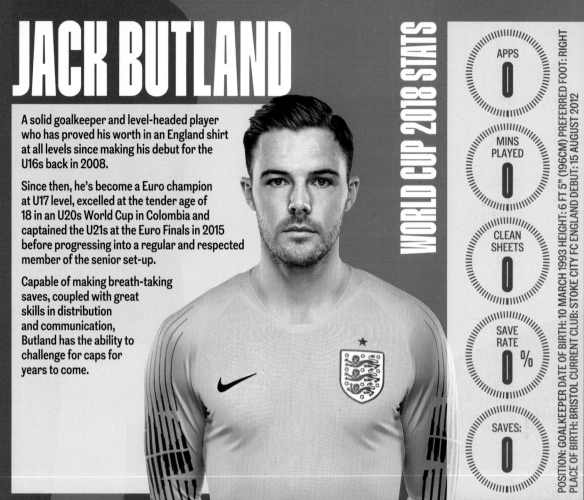

A solid goalkeeper and level-headed player who has proved his worth in an England shirt at all levels since making his debut for the U16s back in 2008.

Since then, he's become a Euro champion at U17 level, excelled at the tender age of 18 in an U20s World Cup in Colombia and captained the U21s at the Euro Finals in 2015 before progressing into a regular and respected member of the senior set-up.

Capable of making breath-taking saves, coupled with great skills in distribution and communication, Butland has the ability to challenge for caps for years to come.

NICK POPE

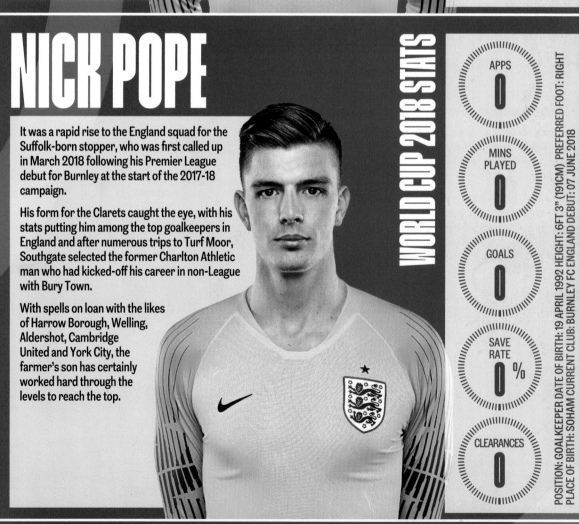

It was a rapid rise to the England squad for the Suffolk-born stopper, who was first called up in March 2018 following his Premier League debut for Burnley at the start of the 2017-18 campaign.

His form for the Clarets caught the eye, with his stats putting him among the top goalkeepers in England and after numerous trips to Turf Moor, Southgate selected the former Charlton Athletic man who had kicked-off his career in non-League with Bury Town.

With spells on loan with the likes of Harrow Borough, Welling, Aldershot, Cambridge United and York City, the farmer's son has certainly worked hard through the levels to reach the top.

TRENT ALEXANDER-ARNOLD

2017-18 was the breakthrough campaign for the Liverpool youngster, who was given a first-team berth at Anfield by Jurgen Klopp and quickly became a regular at right-back for his hometown club.

After working his way through the international ranks with the Young Lions, featuring at the U17 World Cup in Chile in 2015 and also helping the U19s to qualify for the Euro Finals of 2017, Alexander-Arnold became a key man for the U21s before making the senior step.

His first call-up from Gareth Southgate came for the 2018 World Cup, after a stunning end to his domestic campaign with Liverpool by reaching the Champions League Final.

APPS 1
MINS PLAYED 79
GOALS 0
TACKLES 0
CLEARANCES 2

POSITION: DEFENDER DATE OF BIRTH: 07 OCTOBER 1998 HEIGHT: 5FT 9" (175CM) PREFERRED FOOT: RIGHT
PLACE OF BIRTH: LIVERPOOL CURRENT CLUB: LIVERPOOL FC ENGLAND DEBUT: 07 JUNE 2018

GARY CAHILL

There's not much in the domestic game which the Chelsea man hasn't won and he's been an England regular throughout his time at Stamford Bridge.

A tough-tackling and solid presence at the back as well as a capable ball-player and aerial presence in attack, former Aston Villa and Bolton Wanderers player Cahill has been a reliable performer for the Three Lions since his debut against Bulgaria in 2010.

An unfortunately timed injury suffered in a warm-up game with Belgium kept him out of Euro 2012, but he's since represented England in the 2014 World Cup and Euro 2016.

APPS 1
MINS PLAYED 90
GOALS 0
TACKLES 0
CLEARANCES 1

POSITION: DEFENDER DATE OF BIRTH: 19 DECEMBER 1985 HEIGHT: 6FT 4" (193CM) PREFERRED FOOT: RIGHT
PLACE OF BIRTH: DRONFIELD CURRENT CLUB: CHELSEA FC ENGLAND DEBUT: 03 SEPTEMBER 2010

PHIL JONES

A committed and versatile performer for both club and country, the Manchester United man can fill in across the back line and in midfield and brings a whole-hearted attitude and aggressive line to the team.

After starting out as a youngster with Blackburn Rovers under the tutelage of Sam Allardyce and earning caps for England at U19 and U21 level, Jones' performances quickly had scouts flocking to Ewood Park before United won the race for his signature in 2011.

He's since gone on to become a firm favourite at Old Trafford as well as on social media thanks to some eye-catching imagery of him in action illustrating his determination and utter concentration on the game.

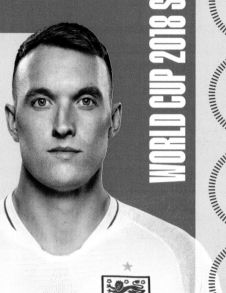

WORLD CUP 2018 STATS

APPS
2

MINS PLAYED
180

GOALS
0

TACKLES
2

CLEARANCES
4

POSITION: DEFENDER DATE OF BIRTH: 21 FEBRUARY 1992 HEIGHT: 5FT 11" (180CM) PREFERRED FOOT: RIGHT
PLACE OF BIRTH: PRESTON CURRENT CLUB: MANCHESTER UNITED FC ENGLAND DEBUT: 07 OCTOBER 2011

HARRY MAGUIRE

A classy defender who first earned his place in the England squad in late 2017, after catching the eye with his form for Leicester City.

Prior to that, Maguire had kick-started his career with boyhood club Sheffield United where he found himself in the first-team as a teenager with the Blades in League One.

A move to Hull City followed and despite finding opportunities hard to come by in his first year on Humberside, he followed that up by captaining the Tigers to promotion and then getting his first taste of the Premier League.

Having made a single appearance for England U21s against Northern Ireland in 2012 during his Bramall Lane days, his senior England debut came in the final World Cup 2018 qualifier with Lithuania almost six years later.

WORLD CUP 2018 STATS

APPS
7

MINS PLAYED
645

GOALS
1

TACKLES
4

CLEARANCES
19

POSITION: DEFENDER DATE OF BIRTH: 05 MARCH 1993 HEIGHT: 6FT 4" (194CM) PREFERRED FOOT: RIGHT
PLACE OF BIRTH: SHEFFIELD CURRENT CLUB: LEICESTER CITY FC ENGLAND DEBUT: 08 OCTOBER 2017

DANNY ROSE

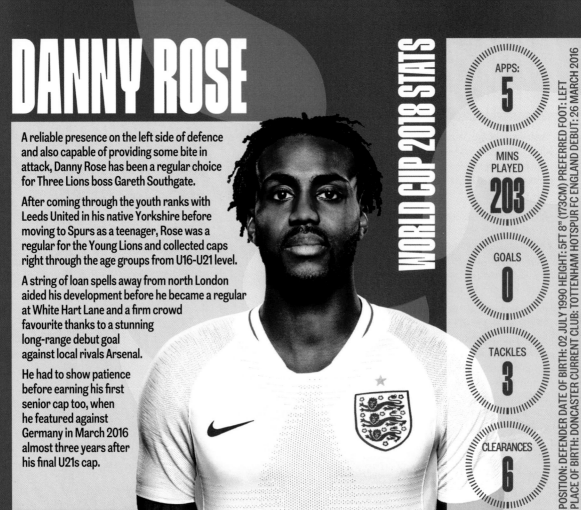

A reliable presence on the left side of defence and also capable of providing some bite in attack, Danny Rose has been a regular choice for Three Lions boss Gareth Southgate.

After coming through the youth ranks with Leeds United in his native Yorkshire before moving to Spurs as a teenager, Rose was a regular for the Young Lions and collected caps right through the age groups from U16-U21 level.

A string of loan spells away from north London aided his development before he became a regular at White Hart Lane and a firm crowd favourite thanks to a stunning long-range debut goal against local rivals Arsenal.

He had to show patience before earning his first senior cap too, when he featured against Germany in March 2016 almost three years after his final U21s cap.

WORLD CUP 2018 STATS

APPS: **5**

MINS PLAYED **203**

GOALS **0**

TACKLES **3**

CLEARANCES **6**

POSITION: DEFENDER DATE OF BIRTH: 02 JULY 1990 HEIGHT: 5FT 8" (173CM) PREFERRED FOOT: LEFT
PLACE OF BIRTH: DONCASTER CURRENT CLUB: TOTTENHAM HOTSPUR FC ENGLAND DEBUT: 26 MARCH 2016

JOHN STONES

A stylish, ball-playing defender, who kicked off his career as a trainee with hometown club Barnsley and worked his way through the England ranks from U19, U20 and U21 level to become a regular in the senior squad by 2015.

With an athletic build, Stones is strong and quick and coupled with his ability on the ball he was playing first-team football with the Tykes at the age of 17 before moving on to Everton in 2013.

His development continued apace there, before a switch to Manchester City in 2016 saw him working under Pep Guardiola and adding more confidence to his game.

WORLD CUP 2018 STATS

APPS: **1**

MINS PLAYED **645**

GOALS **2**

TACKLES **3**

CLEARANCES **31**

POSITION: DEFENDER DATE OF BIRTH: 28 MAY 1994 HEIGHT: 6FT 2" (188CM) PREFERRED FOOT: RIGHT
PLACE OF BIRTH: BARNSLEY CURRENT CLUB: MANCHESTER CITY FC ENGLAND DEBUT: 30 MAY 2014

KIERAN TRIPPIER

The Tottenham Hotspur defender encompasses everything required of the modern full-back, with a tigerish tenacity in the tackle, electric pace and ability to provide crosses and, ultimately, assists.

Born and raised in Bury, Lancashire, Trippier started out with Manchester City where he won the FA Youth Cup in 2008. From there, he made the short trip to Burnley where regular first-team football under the likes of Eddie Howe and Sean Dyche accelerated his progression as he helped the Clarets into the Premier League in 2014.

An England regular at youth level, where he was part of the U19 team which reached the Euro Final of 2009 and also played for the U20s and U21s, he had to wait until June 2017 to make his senior debut when he played against France in Paris.

WORLD CUP 2018 STATS

APPS
6

MINS PLAYED
580

GOALS
1

TACKLES
2

CLEARANCES
11

POSITION: DEFENDER DATE OF BIRTH: 19 SEPTEMBER 1990 HEIGHT: 5FT 10" (178CM) PREFERRED FOOT: RIGHT PLACE OF BIRTH: BURY CURRENT CLUB: TOTTENHAM HOTSPUR FC ENGLAND DEBUT: 13 JUNE 2017

KYLE WALKER

A marauding right-sided defender with an imposing physique and bags of pace who has become an indispensable player for both England and Manchester City.

A native of Sheffield, he began his career as a teenager with the Steel City's United, before sealing a move to Tottenham Hotspur in 2009 and spending eight years with the north London club. There, he honed his talent in the top flight before a switch to Manchester City in 2017 saw him pick up his first Premier League title.

Having featured for England at U19 and U21 level, when he excelled in their respective Euro Finals of 2009 and 2011, he made his senior debut against Spain in November 2011.

WORLD CUP 2018 STATS

APPS
5

MINS PLAYED
495

GOALS
0

TACKLES
1

CLEARANCES
31

POSITION: DEFENDER DATE OF BIRTH: 28 MAY 1990 HEIGHT: 5FT 10" (178CM) PREFERRED FOOT: RIGHT PLACE OF BIRTH: SHEFFIELD CURRENT CLUB: MANCHESTER CITY FC ENGLAND DEBUT: 12 NOVEMBER 2011

ASHLEY YOUNG

The Manchester United man re-emerged as an England player in 2017, following an impressive stint as a left-back at Old Trafford, having previously won 30 caps as a midfielder.

His recall for the games with Germany and Brazil came four years after his previous appearance in 2013 too, with the former Watford and Aston Villa man having previously stated he'd never given up working hard to play for the Three Lions again.

A dab hand from set-plays and full of pace, Young's determination and re-invention as a full-back typifies his attitude and commitment for both club and country.

POSITION: DEFENDER DATE OF BIRTH: 09 JULY 1985 HEIGHT: 5FT 9" (175CM) PREFERRED FOOT: BOTH
PLACE OF BIRTH: STEVENAGE CURRENT CLUB: MANCHESTER UNITED FC ENGLAND DEBUT: 16 NOVEMBER 2007

WORLD CUP 2018 STATS

- APPS: **5**
- MINS PLAYED **462**
- GOALS **0**
- TACKLES **4**
- CLEARANCES **5**

DELE ALLI

A creative spark in the Three Lions midfield, the maestro from Milton Keynes first burst onto the international scene in November 2015 when he scored a stunning long-range goal at Wembley in a victory over France.

He went on to star in Euro 2016 and helped England to sail through qualification for the 2018 World Cup whilst continuing to catch the eye with his performances for Tottenham Hotspur in the Premier League.

Despite his tender years, Alli's rise has been one of hard work and determination after starting out with hometown club MK Dons, cutting his teeth in League One and Two as a teenager before catching the eye of Spurs scouts and making the move to north London.

POSITION: MIDFIELDER DATE OF BIRTH: 11 APRIL 1996 HEIGHT: 6FT 2" (188CM) PREFERRED FOOT: RIGHT
PLACE OF BIRTH: MILTON KEYNES CURRENT CLUB: TOTTENHAM HOTSPUR FC ENGLAND DEBUT: 09 OCTOBER 2015

WORLD CUP 2018 STATS

- APPS: **5**
- MINS PLAYED **364**
- GOALS **1**
- PASSES **151**
- CLEARANCES **0**

FABIAN DELPH

The versatile Yorkshireman provides a variety of options in any squad, with the ability to fill a number of positions whether that's in defence or midfield.

It was as a left-back that Delph excelled during the 2017-18 campaign with a record-breaking Manchester City team, after shaking off an injury-strewn season before that.

Hailing from Bradford, Delph started his career as a dynamic midfielder with Leeds United where he earned caps for England at U19 and U21 level before switching to the top flight with Aston Villa.

WORLD CUP 2018 STATS

APPS
2

MINS PLAYED
220

GOALS
0

TACKLES
4

CLEARANCES
2

POSITION: MIDFIELDER DATE OF BIRTH: 21 NOVEMBER 1989 HEIGHT: 5FT 9" (174CM) PREFERRED FOOT: LEFT
PLACE OF BIRTH: BRADFORD CURRENT CLUB: MANCHESTER CITY FC ENGLAND DEBUT: 03 SEPTEMBER 2014

ERIC DIER

A strong and steadying influence on any team in which he plays, the versatile midfielder is just as comfortable playing as a centre-half as he is in the engine room and has become a key player in the England squad.

Dier, grandson of former FA secretary Ted Croker, moved to Portugal as a youngster with his parents involved in the organisation of Euro 2004 and after showing his ability in the local school leagues in the Algarve, he was picked up by Sporting Lisbon. There, he climbed through the ranks and into the club's senior set-up whilst still being involved in England's development teams following his debut for the U18s in 2011.

A switch to Spurs brought him back to his homeland in 2014 and under the guidance of Mauricio Pochettino, he's become one of the Premier League's top midfielders and has captained both club and country on numerous occasions.

WORLD CUP 2018 STATS

APPS
6

MINS PLAYED
248

GOALS
0

PASSES
193

TACKLES
4

POSITION: MIDFIELDER DATE OF BIRTH: 15 JANUARY 1994 HEIGHT: 6FT 2" (188CM) PREFERRED FOOT: RIGHT
PLACE OF BIRTH: CHELTENHAM CURRENT CLUB: TOTTENHAM HOTSPUR FC ENGLAND DEBUT: 13 NOVEMBER 2015

JORDAN HENDERSON

A favourite son of Sunderland, and a robust and reliable part of both England and Liverpool's midfield which has seen him become a Three Lions regular.

With a good range of passing and intelligent link play, Henderson's never-say-die attitude and commitment to the cause mean he's one of England's leading players in the centre.

A former captain of England U21s, Henderson started off his career with his hometown club where his top-flight form saw him head to Anfield in 2011. His development continued on Merseyside, playing alongside former England captain Steven Gerrard before taking on the Reds' captaincy following his departure.

WORLD CUP 2018 STATS

APPS
5

MINS PLAYED
482

GOALS
0

PASSES
278

TACKLES
1

POSITION: MIDFIELDER DATE OF BIRTH: 17 JUNE 1990 HEIGHT: 6FT 0" (182CM) PREFERRED FOOT: RIGHT
PLACE OF BIRTH: SUNDERLAND CURRENT CLUB: LIVERPOOL FC ENGLAND DEBUT: 17 NOVEMBER 2010

JESSE LINGARD

A firm favourite of Gareth Southgate, right back from their time together with England U21s when the Manchester United livewire was a regular in midfield for the Young Lions.

Capable of running at the opposition with the ball and equally dangerous if presented with a shooting opportunity, Lingard has shown patience and commitment in his development on the way to becoming a first-team player with both club and country.

Something of a lucky charm on England's home patch of Wembley, where he's scored memorable goals for United, the winner in the 2016 FA Cup Final and in the 2017 EFL Cup Final win over Southampton, in particular.

WORLD CUP 2018 STATS

APPS
6

MINS PLAYED
527

GOALS
1

PASSES
227

TACKLES
1

POSITION: MIDFIELDER DATE OF BIRTH: 15 DECEMBER 1992 HEIGHT: 5FT 9" (175CM) PREFERRED FOOT: RIGHT
PLACE OF BIRTH: WARRINGTON CURRENT CLUB: MANCHESTER UNITED FC ENGLAND DEBUT: 08 OCTOBER 2016

RUBEN LOFTUS-CHEEK

Tall, rangy, technical and powerful, the sight of Ruben Loftus-Cheek in full flight is one to behold and having worked closely with the Chelsea youngster from 2015 onwards, England boss Gareth Southgate knows what he's getting.

An impressive senior debut against Germany at Wembley in November 2017 saw the south London lad launch himself into contention for the World Cup in Russia, having previously starred for Southgate's U21s.

His rise through the ranks hasn't been without its setbacks though, with growing pains restricting his earlier appearances for both club and country before he could really strut his stuff in the Premier League during a loan spell with Crystal Palace in 2017-18.

WORLD CUP 2018 STATS

APPS
4

MINS PLAYED
274

GOALS
0

TACKLES
1

PASSES
122

POSITION: MIDFIELDER DATE OF BIRTH: 23 JANUARY 1996 HEIGHT: 6FT 3" (191CM) PREFERRED FOOT: RIGHT
PLACE OF BIRTH: LONDON CURRENT CLUB: CHELSEA FC ENGLAND DEBUT: 10 NOVEMBER 2017

HARRY KANE

England's striking talisman and captain has barely looked back since the moment he scored his first senior goal, just seconds into his debut as a Wembley substitute against Lithuania in March 2015.

The Tottenham Hotspur star had always shown his eye for goal in the formative years of his career, whether that was during his appearances with various Young Lions teams or when out on loan with the likes of Leyton Orient and Millwall.

A strong all-rounder, the east Londoner is clinical with either foot and scores his share of headers, as well as possessing an ability to hold the ball up and bring others into play.

WORLD CUP 2018 STATS

APPS
6

MINS PLAYED
573

GOALS
6

SHOTS
14

PASSES
136

POSITION: FORWARD DATE OF BIRTH: 28 JULY 1993 HEIGHT: 6FT 2" (188CM) PREFERRED FOOT: RIGHT
PLACE OF BIRTH: LONDON CURRENT CLUB: TOTTENHAM HOTSPUR FC ENGLAND DEBUT: 27 MARCH 2015

MARCUS RASHFORD

The Manchester United hotshot enjoyed a whirlwind rise in the 2015-16 campaign, when he came swiftly through the ranks with both club and country.

It all started with a brace on his debut for his hometown club after being thrown into the United line-up to face FC Midtjylland in the Europa League by then Reds boss Louis Van Gaal. Further debut goals followed in the Premier League and FA Cup and on his England senior bow, before he made the step up to the England squad for Euro 2016, all less than four months after his United breakthrough.

A pacy, hard-working and skilful player, Rashford hasn't been far away from the Three Lions squad since then and is a player who loves to get the crowd on their feet with his direct runs, ability to beat players and explosive finishing.

APPS
6

MINS PLAYED
211

GOALS
0

SHOTS
5

PASSES
85

POSITION: FORWARD DATE OF BIRTH: 31 OCTOBER 1997 HEIGHT: 5FT 11" (180CM) PREFERRED FOOT: RIGHT
PLACE OF BIRTH: MANCHESTER CURRENT CLUB: MANCHESTER UNITED FC ENGLAND DEBUT: 27 MAY 2016

RAHEEM STERLING

After growing up in the shadow of Wembley Stadium and sporting a tattoo of the Arch on his arm, it's no surprise the Manchester City flier finds himself at home at the national stadium.

He was first discovered playing in north-west London by QPR, where his ability and reputation grew to the extent that he was said to be on the verge of a first-team call-up at the age of 15 before Liverpool swooped to take him to Anfield.

And it was on Merseyside where he started to make waves, with his tricks, skill and pace putting him in the spotlight as he quickly broke through England's development teams and into the senior set-up, when he made his debut in a game with Sweden in November 2012.

Scoring in a World Cup isn't a new sensation for Sterling, he memorably scored a stunning strike for England against Rwanda at the 2011 U17 World Cup in Mexico.

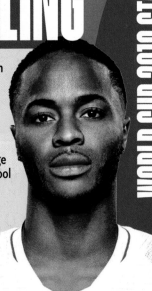

APPS:
6

MINS PLAYED
454

GOALS
0

SHOTS
10

PASSES
130

POSITION: FORWARD DATE OF BIRTH: 08 DECEMBER 1994 HEIGHT: 5FT 7" (170CM) PREFERRED FOOT: BOTH
PLACE OF BIRTH: KINGSTON CURRENT CLUB: MANCHESTER CITY FC ENGLAND DEBUT: 14 NOVEMBER 2012

JAMIE VARDY

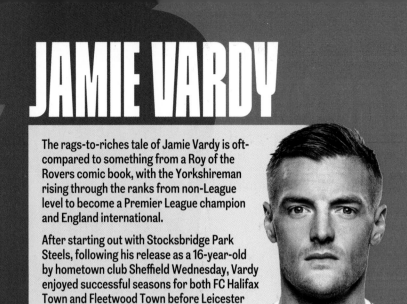

The rags-to-riches tale of Jamie Vardy is oft-compared to something from a Roy of the Rovers comic book, with the Yorkshireman rising through the ranks from non-League level to become a Premier League champion and England international.

After starting out with Stocksbridge Park Steels, following his release as a 16-year-old by hometown club Sheffield Wednesday, Vardy enjoyed successful seasons for both FC Halifax Town and Fleetwood Town before Leicester City took the plunge to sign him.

The whirlwind rise continued as he helped the Foxes into the Premier League and was then a mainstay of the side which upset the odds to win the title in 2016 as well as heading to the Euro Finals in France later that summer.

WORLD CUP 2018 STATS

APPS
4

MINS PLAYED
157

GOALS
0

SHOTS
2

PASSES
22

POSITION: FORWARD DATE OF BIRTH: 11 JANUARY 1987 HEIGHT: 5FT 10" (179CM) PREFERRED FOOT: RIGHT
PLACE OF BIRTH: SHEFFIELD CURRENT CLUB: LEICESTER CITY FC ENGLAND DEBUT: 07 JUNE 2015

DANNY WELBECK

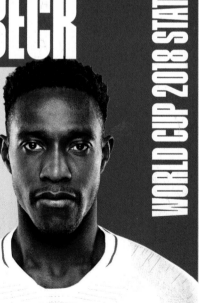

A popular member of the Three Lions squad and a technically gifted forward, capable of causing problems with his pace, movement, ability on the ball and the all-important knack of scoring goals.

He started out as a youngster with hometown club Manchester United having come through their academy since the age of eight and then progressing to the first-team ranks as well as picking up caps with England throughout the age groups, including a trip to the U17 World Cup of 2008 in South Korea.

His senior debut came in a Wembley clash against Ghana, the country of his parents, and as his career took him south to Arsenal he's remained an England regular under the likes of Fabio Capello, Roy Hodgson and Gareth Southgate.

WORLD CUP 2018 STATS

APPS
1

MINS PLAYED
11

GOALS
0

SHOTS
2

PASSES
1

POSITION: FORWARD DATE OF BIRTH: 26 NOVEMBER 1990 HEIGHT: 6FT 1" (185CM) PREFERRED FOOT: RIGHT
PLACE OF BIRTH: MANCHESTER CURRENT CLUB: ARSENAL FC ENGLAND DEBUT: 29 MARCH 2011

WORDSEARCH

Find the words in the grid. Words can go horizontally,
vertically and diagonally in all eight directions.

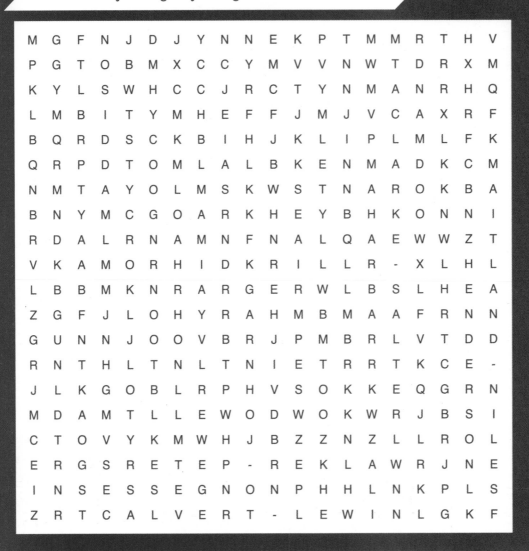

```
M G F N J D J Y N N E K P T M M R T H V
P G T O B M X C C Y M V V N W T D R X M
K Y L S W H C C J R C T Y N M A N R H Q
L M B I T Y M H E F F J M J V C A X R F
B Q R D S C K B I H J K L I P L M L F K
Q R P D T O M L A L B K E N M A D K C M
N M T A Y O L M S K W S T N A R O K B A
B N Y M C G O A R K H E Y B H K O N N I
R D A L R N A M N F N A L Q A E W W Z T
V K A M O R H I D K R I L L R - X L H L
L B B M K N R A R G E R W L B S L H E A
Z G F J L O H Y R A H M B M A A F R N N
G U N N J O O V B R J P M B R L V T D D
R N T H L T N L T N I E T R R T K C E -
J L K G O B L R P H V S O K K E Q G R N
M D A M T L L E W O D W O K W R J B S I
C T O V Y K M W H J B Z Z N Z L L R O L
E R G S R E T E P - R E K L A W R J N E
I N S E S S E G N O N P H H L N K P L S
Z R T C A L V E R T - L E W I N L G K F
```

Abraham	Gray	Onomah
Balcombe	Gunn	Sessegnon
Calvert-Lewin	Harrison	Solanke
Chilwell	Henderson	Tomori
Clarke-Salter	Holgate	Walker-Peters
Davies	Kenny	Winks
Dowell	Lookman	Woodman
Ejaria	Maddison	Worrall
Fry	Maitland-Niles	

Answers on p.61

NAME THE TEAM!

Can you name the England team that started against Panama at World Cup 2018? We've given you one to get you started!

1.
Clue: Goalkeeper – Everton

2.
Clue: Defender – Man. City

3.
Clue: Defender – Man. City

4.
Clue: Defender – Leicester

5.
Clue: Midfielder – Liverpool

6.
Clue: Defender – Tottenham

7.
Clue: Midfielder – Man. United

Ruben Loftus-Cheek
Clue: Midfielder – Chelsea

8.
Clue: Defender – Man. United

9.
Clue: Midfielder – Man. City

10.
Clue: Striker – Tottenham

Answers on p.61

ENGLAND'S GREATEST ALL-TIME XI

England had some great performers at the World Cup, but would any of them make the best all-time greatest XI just yet? Check out who we think might be in it!

GOALKEEPER
Gordon Banks

England has had some great No.1s, but Gordon Banks is surely the best. Banks played 73 times for England and put in loads of outstanding displays in goal – most notably during England's World Cup-winning campaign in 1966.

Also considered: Peter Shilton, David Seaman

Did you know?
Banks made one of the best saves ever against Pele in the 1970 World Cup!

RIGHT-BACK
Gary Neville

Neville was one of the best right-backs of his generation and the best England has produced. He played 85 games for the Three Lions and had an excellent reading of the game, fantastic work-rate, and a tough-tackling style.

Also considered: George Cohen, Jimmy Armfield

Did you know?
England won 44 of the 85 internationals Gary played in.

CENTRE-BACK
Bobby Moore

England's greatest ever defender. Moore captained England to their first and only World Cup triumph, earned a total of 108 caps and was a real leader and hero for his country. The first name on the team-sheet.

Also considered: Des Walker, Rio Ferdinand

Did you know?
There's a statue of the England legend right outside Wembley Stadium!

CENTRE-BACK
John Terry

Terry was without doubt one of the greatest defenders England has ever produced. The Chelsea legend was a rock at the back – strong, commanding and tough, a real leader and an excellent reader of the game.

Also considered: Jack Charlton, Terry Butcher

Did you know?
The defender captained the senior team on 32 occasions

LEFT-BACK
Ashley Cole

The former Arsenal and Chelsea man made 107 appearances for England in an international career spanning 13 years. Impeccable positioning, blistering pace and an ability to cut out danger made him one of England's most reliable defenders ever.

Also considered: Kenny Sansom, Stuart Pearce

Did you know?
Cole is the most capped England full-back of all time with 107 caps.

CENTRE MIDFIELD
Bryan Robson

Robson was the complete midfielder. He could pass, tackle, score, was strong in the air and was superb both on and off the ball. The midfield dynamo was capped 90 times for England, captaining the side 65 times and scoring 26 goals.

Also considered: Nobby Stiles, Alan Ball

Did you know?
Robson was in the starting XI in all of his 90 appearances.

CENTRE MIDFIELD
Paul Gascoigne

Gascoigne earned a total of 57 caps during his England career, and has been described by many as the most naturally gifted English midfielder ever. Gazza was hard, gritty, and passionate, but above all, he had tremendous technical ability.

Also considered: Paul Scholes, Duncan Edwards

Did you know?
Gazza was named in the 1990 World Cup Team Of The Tournament.

RIGHT MIDFIELD
Sir Stanley Matthews

Matthews is arguably the most gifted winger England has ever had. Matthews was a magician – a tricky winger who possessed the quick feet, skill and balance to beat any defender he came up against.

Also considered: David Beckham, Ron Flowers

Did you know?
Matthews holds the record for being the oldest player ever to play for England.

ATTACKING MIDFIELD
Sir Bobby Charlton

Another vital part of England's 1966 World Cup success, Charlton is a true legend of the English game. Until recently, Sir Bobby was England's all-time leading goalscorer, netting 49 goals in 106 appearances.

Also considered: Martin Peters, Frank Lampard

Did you know?
Sir Bobby was part of four World Cup squads, from 1958 to 1970.

LEFT MIDFIELD
Tom Finney

Finney was undoubtedly one of the finest attacking players of the game's post-war years. He played a total of 76 games for England, scoring 30 goals and creating many more for his team-mates.

Also considered: John Barnes, Chris Waddle

Did you know?
The winger was known as 'The Preston Plumber'.

STRIKER
Gary Lineker

Lineker was a born goalscorer. As well as 48 goals in 80 games for the Three Lions, he also won the World Cup Golden Boot in 1986 and is England's all-time top scorer in the World Cup with ten goals from just 12 games.

Also considered: Jimmy Greaves, Alan Shearer, Wayne Rooney

Did you know?
The striker was never booked in his club or international career.

4-2-3-1 FORMATION

BANKS

NEVILLE   MOORE   TERRY   COLE

GASCOIGNE   ROBSON

MATTHEWS   CHARLTON   FINNEY

LINEKER

ENGLAND... ANAGRAMS!

Can you rearrange the jumbled-up letters to reveal the England stars?

1. RAHRY AKNE

2. OHNJ NOTSES

3. HEALYS NOGUY

4. KINARE RITPIPER

5. SUMRAC RODSHARF

6. JANROD SHEERDONN

7. YELK RAWLEK

8. MAJEI DARVY

9. HEERAM STINGERL

10. GRAY ICHALL

Answers on p.61

38

FLASHBACK!

How much do you remember about the England v Colombia round of 16 match at the 2018 World Cup?

1. Where was the round of 16 match played – Moscow, St Petersburg or Kaliningrad?

2. What was the score at half-time?

3. Who scored England's penalty during normal time?

4. How many penalties did England score in the shoot-out?

5. Which player scored the winning penalty for the Three Lions?

Answers on p.61

THE UEFA NATIONS LEAGUE REVEALED!

UEFA NATIONS LEAGUE™

England kicked off their UEFA Nations League campaign in September, but what do you really know about it? Find out all the details here...

WHAT IS IT?

The UEFA Nations League is a competition between the 55 member nations of UEFA. It was created because UEFA and its associations wanted more meaningful fixtures in national team football, with the general feeling that friendly matches weren't providing enough competition for national teams.

SO DOES THAT MEAN THERE WON'T BE ANY MORE FRIENDLIES?

There will be fewer, though there are still a couple of spaces in the calendar. However, Euro 2020 qualifying takes place through March, June, September, October and November 2019, with two games each month, so the majority of teams will not have free international dates for other friendlies next year.

WHAT FORMAT DOES IT TAKE?

The 55 nations were split into four 'Leagues'. The strongest nations are in League A, and the weakest in League D.

Leagues A and B:
Four groups of three nations (12 teams)

League C:
Three groups of four nations, and one group of three (15)

League D:
Four groups of four nations (16)

Teams within each group play each other home and away over the three international weeks in September, October and November.

England is in League A, and they were drawn in a group with Spain and Croatia. The other teams in League A were drawn in the following groups:

LEAGUE A

GROUP 1	GROUP 2	GROUP 3	GROUP 4
Germany	Belgium	Portugal	Spain
France	Switzerland	Italy	England
Holland	Iceland	Poland	Croatia

LEAGUE B

GROUP 1	GROUP 2	GROUP 3	GROUP 4
Slovakia	Russia	Austria	Wales
Ukraine	Sweden	Bosnia and Herzegovina	Republic of Ireland
Czech Republic	Turkey	Northern Ireland	Denmark

LEAGUE C

GROUP 1	GROUP 2	GROUP 3	GROUP 4
Scotland	Hungary	Slovenia	Romania
Albania	Greece	Norway	Serbia
Israel	Finland	Bulgaria	Montenegro
	Estonia	Cyprus	Lithuania

LEAGUE D

GROUP 1	GROUP 2	GROUP 3	GROUP 4
Georgia	Belarus	Azerbaijan	Macedonia
Latvia	Luxembourg	Faroe Islands	Armenia
Kazakhstan	Moldova	Malta	Liechtenstein
Andorra	San Marino	Kosovo	Gibraltar

WILL THERE BE PROMOTION AND RELEGATION?

Yes. The winners of each group in Leagues B, C and D will move up, while the nations bottom of Leagues A, B and C will drop down for the next edition of the Nations League.

WILL THERE ACTUALLY BE UEFA NATIONS LEAGUE CHAMPIONS?

Yes. The four group winners from League A will play off in knockout format – semi-finals, third-place match and final – in June 2019. All four matches will be played in one host European country (to be confirmed). Only nations in League A can go on to be champions.

Finals draw: Early December 2018
Finals: June 5-9, 2019

WHY IS THE UEFA NATIONS LEAGUE IMPORTANT?

Firstly, it will decide each nation's ranking for the Euro 2020 qualifying draw, so ten of the 12 nations in League A are guaranteed to be top seeds, but Leagues B and C will each split almost down the middle to create the lower ranked pots.

Also, there is the 'second chance' via the Euro 2020 play-offs as another carrot, creating a safety net if your qualifying campaign goes badly wrong.

IS THE COMPETITION A ONE-OFF?

No, the next Nations League is due to begin in September 2020, with new divisions based on promotion and relegation, though there is no information at present about how this could affect qualifying for the 2022 World Cup.

EURO 2020 COMES TO WEMBLEY!

The European Championships are changing – did you know the semi-finals and the final of Euro 2020 will be played at Wembley Stadium? Find out more here...

WHAT'S HAPPENING?

UEFA Euro 2020 will mark the 60th anniversary of the competition in style, with 24 teams taking part in a tournament that will be held across 12 different European cities. Unlike previous Euros, there will be no automatic qualifiers, so even countries with host cities will have to earn their place at the finals.

HOW DOES QUALIFYING WORK?

Qualifying has been streamlined, too. The European qualifiers group stage will consist of groups of five or six teams. The group matches will be played between March and November 2019. The winner and runner-up in each of the ten groups will make it through, determining the first 20 places at Euro 2020.

THEN WHAT?

The last four Euro places will be won through the European qualifying play-offs, which will be played out by the 16 teams who have qualified through the UEFA Nations League.

The 16 teams will be divided into four groups, which will make four play-off paths. Each one will feature two semi-finals and then a final, to see who qualifies for Euro 2020.

THE EURO 2020 FINALS

The 24 teams who have qualified will be split into six groups of four. The top two in each group will progress to the last 16, along with the four best third-place finishers. From then on, it's a straight knockout competition. And with matches having been played all over Europe, all roads lead to London as the semi-finals and final are being held at Wembley!

WHICH CITIES ARE HOSTING GAMES?

There are 12 cities in all, spread all over Europe. Each city will have certain games in the Euro 2020 group stage, as well as the last 16 and quarter-finals. Wembley is hosting the most matches, including the semi-finals and final. Check out all the host cities below.

CITY	COUNTRY	STADIUM	CAPACITY
Amsterdam	Netherlands	Johan Cruyff Arena	56,000
Baku	Azerbaijan	Olympic Stadium	68,700
Bilbao	Spain	San Mamés	53,289
Bucharest	Romania	Arena Nationala	55,600
Budapest	Hungary	Ferenc Puskás Stadium	38,652
Copenhagen	Denmark	Parken Stadium	51,700
Dublin	Rep. Ireland	Dublin Arena	53,332
Glasgow	Scotland	Hampden Park	52,063
London	England	Wembley Stadium	90,000
Munich	Germany	Allianz Arena Munich	75,000
Rome	Italy	Olympic Stadium	72,698
Saint Petersburg	Russia	Saint Petersburg Stadium	68,134

THE FINAL OF EURO 2020 WILL BE PLAYED ON JULY 12, 2020!

ENGLAND'S NEWEST STARS!

England's youth teams are doing brilliantly right now, with the U20s and U17s both winning their respective World Cups in 2017! Find out more about some of these new heroes who will be fighting for a place in the seniors before long.

RHIAN BREWSTER

Date of Birth: 1 April 2000
Position: Striker
Club: Liverpool

A rapid forward whose finishing is second to none. He scored consecutive hat-tricks in the quarter and semi-finals of the U17s World Cup, and then hit a crucial goal in the final against Spain just before half-time. His goalscoring record for the Young Lions is phenomenal and he's highly rated at Anfield too.

TREVOH CHALOBAH

Date of Birth: 5 July 1999
Position: Centre-back
Club: Ipswich (on loan from Chelsea)

Centre-back or midfielder Chalobah looks mature and composed, with real leadership qualities. He was made captain of the England U19s, despite only turning 18 on the day of England's opening game of the European Championships against Bulgaria. He'll be looking to make an impact in the Championship with Ipswich this season.

PHIL FODEN

Date of Birth: 28 May 2000
Position: Midfielder
Club: Manchester City

Foden enjoyed a sensational U17 World Cup, where he dismantled Brazil in the semis before doing the same to Spain in the final. The Manchester City youngster is a No.10 or winger, who plays with his head up and is superb technically. He cuts defences apart with his passing, can beat players without the need for lots of tricks, and also scores his fair share of goals. His ability caught the eye of Pep Guardiola, who introduced him to the first-team squad with his boyhood club as well as becoming the youngest English player to feature in the Champions League.

EDWARD NKETIAH

Date of Birth: 30 May 1999
Position: Forward
Club: Arsenal

A real penalty box predator, Nketiah doesn't score many goals from outside the area. Instead, he uses his pace to get to the penalty box and his skill to find space for a shot. Him and Reiss Nelson are the players most readily name-checked for a breakthrough to the Arsenal first team and look set to be given more opportunities this season. After an impressive season with the U19s, Nketiah joined the U21s in May 2018 to help them win the Toulon Tournament in France.

BEN BRERETON

Date of Birth: 18 April 1999
Position: Striker
Club: Nottingham Forest

Part of the England U19 squad who won the Euro title in Georgia 2017, when they beat Portugal in the final. Brereton has so many attributes as a striker. He has pace, quick instincts, can score all kinds of goals, is physically strong and has good link-up play. After starting his career with Stoke City, he signed for Forest as a teenager before breaking into their first-team squad.

MARC GUEHI

Date of Birth: 13 July 2000
Position: Centre-back
Club: Chelsea

Guehi was an ever-present in both the Euro and World Cup tournaments for the U17s in 2017. He is a modern defender who is comfortable on the ball, but has a physical presence for opposition attackers, and one who is a threat from set-pieces as shown with his goal in the World Cup Final against Spain.

MASON MOUNT

Date of Birth: 10 January 1999
Position: Midfielder
Club: Chelsea

Another key player who helped England to win the U19 Euros in July 2017. Mount seems to glide effortlessly across the pitch and is a real creative lynchpin, picking out team-mates with this superb vision and range of passing. He's a box-to-box player who is especially effective in the final third of the pitch. Like many Chelsea youngsters, Mount spent 2017-18 on loan at Vitesse Arnhem in Holland.

REISS NELSON

Date of Birth: 10 December 1999
Position: Forward
Club: Arsenal

Nelson is a real box of tricks, has fantastic acceleration and can finish or provide for others, which has been proven by an impressive record for Arsenal U23s and England. He has incredible close control and a frightening ability to change direction at high speed. Last season he saw game time at wing-back for the Arsenal first team, but his future is surely in a role further forward.

JOEL LATIBEAUDIERE

Date of Birth: 6 January 2000
Position: Centre-back
Club: Manchester City

A well-rounded defender who captained the England U17s to World Cup glory in October 2017. His athleticism and composure allow him to particularly excel in defending one-on-one situations, and his commanding presence means he's a comfortable captain and leader.

JONATHAN PANZO

Date of Birth: 25 October 2000
Position: Centre-back
Club: AS Monaco

Panzo is a versatile defender who usually plays at centre-back, but also performed admirably for England U17s at left-back during their World Cup triumph. He is comfortable on the ball and skilful, which helps him play his way out of tight situations. He can find the right pass as well as beat a player and come out with the ball to relieve pressure.

JADON SANCHO

Date of Birth: 25 March 2000
Position: Attacking midfielder
Club: Borussia Dortmund

Following his £8m move from Manchester City to Borussia Dortmund in the summer of 2017, Sancho has broken into their first team and is starting to make a name for himself. A regular for England from U16 through to U19 level, he loves to occupy the left wing from where he uses his blend of devastating speed, skills and finishing to punish opponents. However, no-one can argue with his goalscoring and assist records, especially for England.

CURTIS ANDERSON

Date of Birth: 27 September 2000
Position: Goalkeeper
Club: Manchester City

A key member of the World Cup-winning U17 team of 2017. During the competition in India, he saved a crucial penalty in the shootout against Japan in the round of 16, before stepping up to convert one to helped the Young Lions progress. Anderson is tall, strong and commands his area, as well as being an excellent shot-stopper.

CROSSWORD

Work out the answers using the clues and write them in the crossword!

ACROSS

1 Man City ace who scored two against Panama in the World Cup. (4,6)
4 Age of Marcus Rashford when he made his England debut. (8)
5 The Three Lions' all-time record caps holder. (7)
9 England's former MK Dons hero. (4,4)
10 England's manager in 1966. (3,6)
12 Tottenham star Eric Dier's first club. (8,6)
15 Team England beat 6-1 at World Cup 2018. (6)
17 England's all-time record goalscorer. (6)
18 Club Jamie Vardy won the Premier League with. (9,4)
19 England coach whose name is also a country. (7)

DOWN

2 England's first opponent in the World Cup 2018. (7)
3 Gareth Southgate used to manage this club. (13)
6 Former club of Kyle Walker and Harry Maguire. (9,6)
7 England's first goalscorer at World Cup 2018. (5,4)
8 England's World Cup-winning brothers. (8)
11 England's former Villa and Bolton defender. (4,6)
13 Three Lions' Everton stopper. (8)
14 England's first opponent in the Nations League. (5)
16 England's home stadium. (7)

Answers on p.61

SPOT THE STAR

Can you tell who these Three Lions players are?

1. Answer:

2. Answer:

3. Answer:

4. Answer:

5. Answer:

6. Answer:

7. Answer:

8. Answer:

9. Answer:

Answers on p.61

ENGLAND RECORD BREAKERS!

Check out the England players who have broken all kinds of amazing records!

BIGGEST WORLD CUP FINALS WIN

England's biggest win in the World Cup finals came in 2018! A Harry Kane-inspired Three Lions beat Panama 6-1 thanks to a hat-trick from the captain.

125 Peter Shilton holds the record for the most England appearances – the goalkeeper won 125 caps for the Three Lions. His first came on November 25 1970 against East Germany, while his last was on July 7 1990 in the World Cup third place play-off against Italy!

70 England legend Billy Wright holds the record for the most consecutive appearances. He played in 70 games on the trot, starting with a 2-2 draw with France on October 3 1951 all the way to the 8-1 over USA in Los Angeles on May 28 1959. Better still, he was captain for all of them too!

MOST HAT-TRICKS

Former Tottenham and Chelsea hero Jimmy Greaves holds the record for the most England hat-tricks. He netted a total of six for the Three Lions.

Date	Opponent	Score	Goals
19.10.60	Luxembourg	9-0	3
15.04.61	Scotland	9-3	3
20.06.62	Peru	4-0	3
20.11.63	N. Ireland	8-3	4
03.10.64	N. Ireland	4-3	3
29.10.66	Norway	6-1	4

YOUNGEST PLAYER

On May 30 2006, Theo Walcott became the youngest ever senior player by appearing in the 3-1 win over Hungary at Old Trafford aged just 17 years and 75 days old.

90

England legends Billy Wright and Bobby Moore hold the record for the most appearances as captain – they both skippered the side on 90 occasions.

	Caps	As Captain	Wins
Bobby Moore	108	90	57
Billy Wright	105	90	49

FASTEST GOAL FROM KICK-OFF

In 1947, Tommy Lawton scored for England just 17 seconds after the kick-off against Portugal that ended in a 10-0 win for the Three Lions.

721

Legendary England goalkeeper and World Cup winner Gordon Banks kept seven consecutive clean sheets, and didn't concede for 721 minutes, between April 2 1966 and July 23, 1966.

53 The record for the most England goals belongs to Wayne Rooney. The striker netted 53 goals in 119 games for his country, and beat Sir Bobby Charlton's previous record of 49 with a goal at Wembley against Switzerland on September 8 2015.

APPEARANCES UNDER MOST DIFFERENT MANAGERS

Gareth Barry had a 12-year England senior career between 2002 and 2012, and played under a record eight managers in that time!

Year	Manager
2000	Kevin Keegan
2000	Howard Wilkinson
2000	Peter Taylor
2001-2006	Sven Goran Eriksson
2006-07	Steve McClaren
2008-12	Fabio Capello
2012	Stuart Pearce
2012	Roy Hodgson

BEST GOALS PER GAME

George Camsell holds an unbelievable record of averaging TWO goals per game for England!
The Middlesbrough star scored 18 goals in just nine games for England back in the 1920s and 1930s.

Name	Goals	Games	Goals per game
George Camsell	18	9	2.00
Steve Bloomer	28	23	1.22
Dixie Dean	18	16	1.13
Tommy Lawton	22	23	0.96
Stan Mortensen	23	25	0.92

10

Gary Lineker holds the record for the most goals at World Cup finals – the deadly striker netted ten World Cup goals between 1986 and 1990.

LINEKER'S WORLD CUP GOALS

Date	Opponent	Stage	Goals	Final Score
11.06.86	Poland	Group	3	3-0
18.06.86	Paraguay	Round Of 16	2	3-1
22.06.86	Argentina	Quarter-final	1	1-2
11.06.90	Rep. Ireland	Group	1	1-1
01.07.90	Cameroon	Quarter-final	2	3-1
04.07.90	West Germany	Semi-final	1	1-1*

* England lost on penalties

BIGGEST VICTORY

On February 18, 1882, England played Ireland in Belfast and recorded a 13-0 win, which is still their biggest-ever victory. Aston Villa's Howard Vaughton made his debut that day and scored five goals!

14

Arsenal star David Rocastle played 14 games for England without losing between September 14 1988 and May 17, 1992. That's still a record!

FASTEST GOAL AS A SUBSTITUTE

Former Tottenham and Manchester United striker Teddy Sheringham scored just 15 seconds after coming on as a substitute for England against Greece in the 2-2 draw on October 6, 2001. It's still the fastest goal ever scored by an England substitute.

FIFA WOMEN'S WORLD CUP FRANCE 2019!

Get ready for a massive summer of football in 2019 –
the FIFA Women's World Cup!

WHEN?

The FIFA Women's World Cup kicks off in the Parc Des Princes
in Paris on Friday, June 7. There's then a whole month of epic
World Cup action before the final in Lyon on Sunday, July 7,
where the winners will be crowned World Cup Champions!
Here's a breakdown of when the games are taking place...

GROUP STAGE Friday, June 7 to Thursday, June 20

ROUND OF 16 Saturday, June 22 to Tuesday, June 25

QUARTER-FINALS Thursday, June 27 to Saturday, June 29

SEMI-FINALS Tuesday, July 2 and Wednesday, July 3

THIRD PLACE PLAY-OFF Saturday, July 6

FINAL Sunday, July 7

LE HAVRE
Stade Oceane
Capacity: 25,278

PARIS
Parc Des Princes
Capacity: 48,583

VALENCIENNES
Stade du Hainaut
Capacity: 25,172

REIMS
Stade Auguste-Delaune
Capacity: 19,465

RENNES
Roazhon Park
Capacity: 29,820

LYON
Stade De Lyon
Capacity: 58,215

GRENOBLE
Stade des Alpes
Capacity: 20,068

NICE
Stade De Nice
Capacity: 36,178

MONTPELLIER
Stade de la Mosson
Capacity: 27,310

WHERE?
The FIFA Women's World Cup will be staged at nine venues across France, from Valenciennes in the north, to Montpellier in the south. Check out the stadiums the games will be played at!

PREVIOUS WINNERS

Since the Women's World Cup was first played in 1991, there have been seven tournaments, with four different winners. Here's a breakdown of which country won each competition.

Year	Host	Champions	Score	Runner-up
1991	China	USA	2-1	Norway
1995	Sweden	Norway	2-0	Germany
1999	USA	USA	0-0 (5-4 pens)	China
2003	USA	Germany	2-1	Sweden
2007	China	Germany	2-0	Brazil
2011	Germany	Japan	2-2 (3-1 pens)	USA
2015	Canada	USA	5-2	Japan

WINNERS TABLE

USA   GERMANY   NORWAY   JAPAN

OFFICIAL MASCOT

Ettie is a young chicken with a passion for life and football. She comes from a long line of feathered mascots and is the daughter of Footix, the Official Mascot from the 1998 FIFA World Cup France. Her strong family connection to the Gallic rooster, who is still a popular national French symbol, makes her a fitting choice as the Official Mascot for the FIFA Women's World Cup France 2019.

Ettie's name comes from the French word for star, étoile, as she came from the bright star that her father Footix was awarded for the 1998 FIFA World Cup. Footix cast his star far into the night sky so it could shine brightly, and after a few years of travelling through the cosmos it came back to him in the form of his twinkling daughter, Ettie.

THE SQUAD

Here are the players hoping to take the World Cup by storm in 2019!

COACH: PHIL NEVILLE

The former Manchester United and Everton defender played over 500 games and won six Premier League titles, as well as 59 England caps, during a glittering career. A solid and versatile defender who could operate anywhere in the back four and in midfield, Neville has plenty of coaching experience, having worked with the England Men's Under-21 side as well as Manchester United and Valencia.

DEFENDERS

HANNAH BLUNDELL
Date of Birth:
25 May 1994
Club:
Chelsea

GOALKEEPERS

KAREN BARDSLEY
Date of Birth:
14 October 1984
Club:
Manchester City

MILLIE BRIGHT
Date of Birth:
21 August 1993
Club:
Chelsea

MARY EARPS
Date of Birth:
07 March 1993
Club:
Wolfsburg

LUCY BRONZE
Date of Birth:
28 October 1991
Club:
Lyon

CARLY TELFORD
Date of Birth:
07 July 1987
Club:
Chelsea

RACHEL DALY
Date of Birth:
06 December 1991
Club:
Houston Dash

ALEX GREENWOOD

Date of Birth:
07 September 1993
Club:
Manchester United

GABBY GEORGE

Date of Birth:
02 February 1997
Club:
Everton

MIDFIELDERS

STEPH HOUGHTON

Date of Birth:
23 April 1988
Club:
Manchester City

KAREN CARNEY

Date of Birth:
01 August 1987
Club:
Chelsea

ABBIE McMANUS

Date of Birth:
14 January 1993
Club:
Manchester City

ISOBEL CHRISTIANSEN

Date of Birth:
20 September 1991
Club:
Lyon

DEMI STOKES

Date of Birth:
12 December 1991
Club:
Manchester City

JADE MOORE

Date of Birth:
22 October 1990
Club:
Reading

LEAH WILLIAMSON

Date of Birth:
29 March 1997
Club:
Arsenal

JORDAN NOBBS

Date of Birth:
08 December 1992
Club:
Arsenal

JILL
SCOTT
Date of Birth:
02 February 1987
Club:
Manchester City

MELISSA
LAWLEY
Date of Birth:
28 April 1994
Club:
Manchester City

KEIRA
WALSH
Date of Birth:
08 April 1997
Club:
Manchester City

BETH
MEAD
Date of Birth:
09 May 1995
Club:
Arsenal

FARA
WILLIAMS
Date of Birth:
25 January 1984
Club:
Reading

NIKITA
PARRIS
Date of Birth:
10 March 1994
Club:
Manchester City

FORWARDS

TONI
DUGGAN
Date of Birth:
25 July 1991
Club:
Barcelona

JODIE
TAYLOR
Date of Birth:
17 May 1986
Club:
Seattle Reign

FRAN
KIRBY
Date of Birth:
29 June 1993
Club:
Chelsea

ELLEN
WHITE
Date of Birth:
09 May 1989
Club:
Birmingham City

ANSWERS

How did you get on testing your England knowledge?

Page 12: Wordfit

```
        J   S
        O   T       Y
        N   O       O       W
    K A N E S T O N A U   V A R D Y
        S T E R L I N G   A     I
        S   E       G     L     E
            X             K   R O S E
        A   R A S H F O R D
  C A H I L L     N             W
        L         D             E
    P I C K F O R D             L
        O         R     T       B
        P   L I N G A R D       E
        E     A   R   M A G U I R E
              A   O   I         C
            H E N D E R S O N   K
          D E       O P
          E   L O F T U S C H E E K
    B U T L A N D     I
          P           E
          H           R
```

Page 13: Spot the Difference

Page 14 Room Mates

Jesse on Marcus: Marcus on Jesse:
1. A   1. C
2. B   2. C
3. B   3. A
4. C   4. B
5. A   5. C

Page 18: 20 Questions

1. Wayne Rooney   12. 90,000
2. John Stones   13. Harry Kane
3. Nike   14. 12
4. Once (1966)   15. Welbeck
5. 1990   16. Harry Maguire
6. Harry Kane   17. Kieran Trippier
7. Tottenham   18. Aston Villa
8. One   19. Two
9. All white   20. True
10. Jamie Vardy
11. Peter Shilton

Page 19: Face in the Crowd

Page 38: England Anagrams

1. Harry Kane
2. John Stones
3. Ashley Young
4. Kieran Trippier
5. Marcus Rashford
6. Jordan Henderson
7. Kyle Walker
8. Jamie Vardy
9. Raheem Sterling
10. Gary Cahill

Page 39: Flashback Quiz

1. Moscow
2. 0-0
3. Harry Kane
4. Four
5. Eric Dier

Page 32: Wordsearch

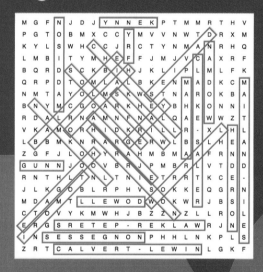

Page 48: Crossword

```
J O H N S T O N E S   M
U         E I G H T E E N
S H I L T O N   S   D
I         H       D
C         E   D E L E A L L I   H
H       A L F R A M S E Y       A
A       O   I       R   B       R
R       N   E       U   R       R
S P O R T I N G L I S B O N   P A N A M A   Y
I       O   D   P   U   W       C
C       N   U   A   G   E       A
K       F   N   I   H   M       H
F         I   T   N     B   I
O R O O N E Y   D       L   L
R                 L E I C E S T E R C I T Y
D                       Y
                        H O L L A N D
```

Page 33: Name the Team

1. Jordan Pickford
2. Kyle Walker
3. John Stones
4. Harry Maguire
5. Jordan Henderson
6. Kieran Trippier
7. Jesse Lingard
8. Ashley Young
9. Raheem Sterling
10. Harry Kane

Page 49: Spot the Star

1. Jordan Henderson
2. John Stones
3. Harry Kane
4. Raheem Sterling
5. Marcus Rashford
6. Dele Alli
7. Jamie Vardy
8. Kyle Walker
9. Gary Cahill